# MOLA DESIGNS

## 45 Authentic Indian Designs from Panama

Frederick W. Shaffer

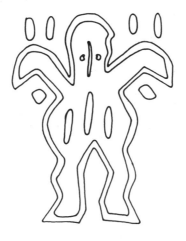

Dover Publications, Inc., New York

**Planet Friendly Publishing**
✔ Made in the United States
✔ Printed on Recycled Paper
Text: 30%     Cover: 10%
Learn more: www.greenedition.org

GREEN EDITION

At Dover Publications we're committed to producing books in an earth-friendly manner and to helping our customers make greener choices.

Manufacturing books in the United States ensures compliance with strict environmental laws and eliminates the need for international freight shipping, a major contributor to global air pollution.

And printing on recycled paper helps minimize our consumption of trees, water and fossil fuels. The text of *Mola Designs* was printed on paper made with 30% post-consumer waste, and the cover was printed on paper made with 10% post-consumer waste. According to Environmental Defense's Paper Calculator, by using this innovative paper instead of conventional papers, we achieved the following environmental benefits:

Trees Saved: 5   •   Air Emissions Eliminated: 394 pounds
Water Saved: 1,610 gallons   •   Solid Waste Eliminated: 210 pounds

For more information on our environmental practices, please visit us online at www.doverpublications.com/green

*Copyright*

*Bibliographical Note*

*Mola Designs: 45 Authentic Indian Designs from Panama*, as published by Dover Publications, Inc., in 1985, is a slightly revised republication, incorporating all 45 designs, of the work originally published by Dover in 1982 under the title *Mola Design Coloring Book*.

DOVER *Pictorial Archive* SERIES

This book belongs to the Dover Pictorial Archive Series. You may use the designs and illustrations for graphics and crafts applications, free and without special permission, provided that you include no more than four in the same publication or project. (For permission for additional use, please write to Permissions Department, Dover Publications, Inc., 31 East 2nd Street, Mineola, N.Y. 11501.)

However, republication or reproduction of any illustration by any other graphic service, whether it be in a book or in any other design resource, is strictly prohibited.

*Library of Congress Cataloging-in-Publication Data*

Shaffer, Frederick W.
    Mola designs.
    Rev. ed. of: Mola design coloring book. 1982
    Summary: Black-and-white designs based on reverse appliqué mola patterns worked by Cuna Indian women in Panama.
    1. Appliqué—Panama—Patterns. 2. Molas—Panama—Patterns. 2. Cuna Indians—Textile industry and fabrics. 4. Indians of Central America—Panama—Textile industry and fabrics. [1. Appliqué—Patterns. 2. Molas—Patterns. 3. Cuna Indians—Textile industry and fabrics. 4. Indians of Central America—Textile industry and fabrics. 5. Coloring books] I. Shaffer, Frederick W. Mola design coloring book. II. Title.

TT779.S45  1985  746.44'5041  85-10303

*International Standard Book Number*
*ISBN-13: 978-0-486-24289-7*
*ISBN-10: 0-486-24289-7*

Manufactured in the United States of America
Dover Publications, Inc., 31 East 2nd Street, Mineola, N.Y. 11501

# Introduction

## The Origin of the Mola

The mola has been around for more than a hundred years. It is a distinctive native craft—colorful, original in concept and design, and intricate in execution—made exclusively by the Cuna (or Kuna) Indians (see Figure 1). As an art object, the mola bears a direct relationship to body painting, practiced past and present, by primitive peoples such as the Carajá Indians of Brazil and the Chocó Indians of the Darién region of Panama. In 1971 I saw Chocó Indian women dressed only in sarong-like skirts. The lower portions of their faces were stained with the purple dye of the genipa plant, which had been applied from just below their earlobes to the corners of their mouths, down over and under the chin to where the chin and neck join. On each breast there were circular or spiral designs. I mention the continuing practice of body painting by the Chocó because this tribe has always been a neighbor of the Cuna, who also practiced body painting until as recently as two hundred seventy years ago.

In the middle of the eighteenth century French Huguenots arrived among the Cuna and the two groups associated closely for over fifty years. It was during this period that the Cuna women began decorating the bottom hemline of their long skirts with a wide variety of designs and symbols, an art form that continued until the middle of the nineteenth century, at which time the wearing of a long, blouse-like garment also became a Cuna fashion. With the gradual change to their present multipiece attire of short blouse, skirt, shawl, and sash, the Cuna women have once again returned symbolic designs to their bodies by way of their colorful molas.

Figure 1. An early form of the mola, circa 1923. Note that one child is an albino. By permission of The Smithsonian Institution, Washington, D.C.

Figure 2. Cuna women performing a ritual dance. By permission of the Panama Government Tourist Bureau.

## The Cuna People

The Cuna Indian people occupy fifty or more of the three-hundred-fifty-odd islands of the San Blas archipelago, which lies off the Atlantic coast of the Isthmus of Panama. Their largest group, some twenty-five thousand, lives in congested communities that cover entire islands. A far smaller number are found in several small towns across the border in Colombia, a remnant of those who lived there when Panama was still a part of Colombia.

The Cuna population is growing, but it is only a fraction of that which once inhabited the area. Old World explorers and exploiters came upon the Cuna during the fifteenth and sixteenth centuries. They captured and enslaved many of them and slaughtered others. Then diseases introduced by these travelers from Europe decimated the Cuna. Worsening living conditions induced the mainland Cuna to seek other areas in which to live. Thus began a more than century-long migration by the majority of the Cuna across the Isthmus of Panama from the Pacific Ocean to the Atlantic. For many of the Cuna, the San Blas Islands became their new home.

The Cuna are noteworthy not only for their attire but for their physical appearance as well (see Figure 2). They are small in stature, with light to medium brown coloration, and have very dark hair and eyes. As a cultural group they seem to have the world's highest incidence of albinism—about 1 percent of the entire population (see Figure 1). The presence of the albinos gave rise to early explorers' tales of a white race of Indians in the Caribbean Islands.

*Figure 3. Feliciana Robler, a young Cuna woman, wearing a mola and jewelry, including a nose ring. By permission of the Panama Government Tourist Bureau.*

The Cuna women wear traditional gold nose rings, necklaces, earrings, and strings of small, brightly colored beads wrapped around their forearms and calves (see Figures 3 and 4). On their cheeks they apply rouge in a circular form. Since the nose is considered an important aspect of a woman's beauty, the Cuna enhance it by penciling a fine line down its center from the bridge to the tip. A brightly colored shawl covers the head and shoulders and is worn with a red or black wraparound skirt—and, of course, the mola blouse.

The Cuna men lack the glitter of their womenfolk. They dress conservatively, usually in white shirt and dark trousers. They are primarily farmers, raising a very large crop of coconuts for export on islands reserved exclusively for farming. The coconut crop provides the Cuna with their major source of income. When the Cuna men are not farming, they produce attractive carved wooden furniture and religious figures.

Some anthropologists believe that the Cuna culture originated in Southeast Asia almost six thousand years ago. It is speculated that when the Cuna came to the Western Hemisphere, they brought with them their religion, rites, customs, designs, and symbols; this might account for the seeming lack of relationship of the Cuna culture to that of any other people of this hemisphere. It has also been suggested that the Cuna could be a remnant of the once numerous Carib Indians of the Caribbean Islands and coastal areas of Central and South America.

Toward the latter part of the nineteenth century, the French began to construct the Panama Canal. During that period the Cuna and the French again lived in close proximity. The Cuna world was almost shattered in 1904, however, when Panama declared its independence from Colombia. Panama claimed all the lands of the isthmus, including some territories that had traditionally been Cuna. Disagreements arose during the 1920s that the Cuna tried to resolve by creating their own nation, the Republic of Tule, and declaring their independence from Panama. Difficult relations persisted between Panama and the Cuna for some time, however, until finally settled through the Porvenir Treaty, which the two peoples signed in 1925. This treaty provided the Cuna with their own bill of rights and control of their government and civil affairs.

*Figure 4. Groups of highly decorated Cuna women. By permission of the Panama Government Tourist Bureau.*

4

## Making a Mola

To make a mola, a Cuna seamstress layers rectangles of brightly colored cotton cloth of good quality (see Figure 5). The average size of the large molas in my personal collection is 18⅞" x 16⅞", with the very largest measuring 20¼" x 18". The layers of fabric are basted together. When all the fabric is securely joined, the seamstress prepares her design.

On the top layer—usually a piece of very bright red, hot orange, or, for contrast, black fabric—a design is drawn in pencil. Once the design is established on the top layer, it and the layers of fabric underneath are cut through with small pointed scissors. The overall design emerges as the process of cutting continues. (Among more experienced mola-makers, the fabric is often cut freehand, without a guiding penciled outline of the design.) With each cut, pieces of cloth are removed and the colors of lower layers show through. The cut edges of the cloth are then carefully folded under and finished with hidden stitches. The procedure of cutting away fabric is called *reverse appliqué*, and is unique to the mola craft. In addition to this specialized needlework, conventional appliqué and embroidery are also employed in almost every mola design.

When a color other than those of the fabric layers is to be introduced, the design element through which the color will show is cut out, a patch of the desired color is inserted under the opening and between the layers, and then the design is sewed down. In such cases the seamstress often will use conventional appliqué to apply yet another color on top of the patch.

Using only hand needlework, a Cuna seamstress ordinarily requires about two months to complete a single panel, during which time she also performs her regular home chores. At the same time she also works on the first panel's mate and several others that will become part of other blouses at a later time. The completed original panel and its mate will be used on the front and back of the mola-maker's own blouse. Although each pair of molas is intended for use on the same blouse, the two panels are seldom identical. Indeed the manner in which they are made almost precludes anything beyond close similarity.

Girls in every Cuna family begin to learn the art of needlework and mola design when they are six or seven years old. Several examples of the small practice mola designs made by young girls are included in this volume. By the time she has reached marriageable age, every young woman will have assembled a score or more blouses that she considers to be the very finest she has ever made. These are highly treasured and given the very greatest care. This special attention is essential in a tropical climate where the elements will normally cause almost any fabric to deteriorate. Early examples of the

*Figure 5. Sewing together the layers of fabric for a mola. By permission of the Panama Government Tourist Bureau.*

craft are difficult to find except in museums and private collections, where they have been cared for under favorable conditions.

## Mola Designs

Designs used in making molas fall within loosely defined categories. Traditional subjects include religion, mythology, superstitions, and Cuna home life. There is extensive use of natural and abstract bird and animal designs. Common among the latter group are snakes, lizards, insects, fish, and other marine life. Many designs also include flowers, geometric figures, and mazes. Some molas display political slogans, advertising layouts, and trademarks of well-known products that have been freely lifted from magazines. Sports such as soccer, basketball, and baseball also find their way into the mola patterns of the present day, as do rockets and space capsules. The current molas possess the general appearance and colors of the traditional ones, but they also demonstrate the extent of the influences of the modern world upon the Cuna way of life.

## A Color Guide

The following colors are those most frequently used

5

in molas. The first group is used almost exclusively for the topmost layer:

Scarlet (or Cadmium Red Light)
Carmine (or Alizarine Crimson)
Orange
Black

The colors used to form the second, third, and other layers of the packet of cloth, as well as other parts of the finished mola, are:

| | |
|---|---|
| Lemon Yellow | Violet |
| Cadmium Yellow Medium | Hooker's Green |
| Yellow Ochre | Emerald Green |
| Orange | Olive Green |
| Cadmium Red Light | Prussian Blue |
| Alizarine Crimson | Black |
| Cerise | White |
| Purple | |

These colors can be used in any pleasing combination. The colors selected by the Cuna seamstresses are crisply bright, but they are always kept in careful balance. Authentically colored versions of the mola designs on pages 8, 9, 13, 14, 16, 17, 18, 25, 32, 34, 35, and 45 appear on the inside and outside covers of this book.

## Sequence of Plates and Captions

The full-page plates appearing on pages 7–45 are organized by theme: home (pages 7–11), religion and superstition (pages 12–15), animal life (pages 16–29), trees and flowers (pages 30–31), and miscellaneous (pages 32–45). The smaller illustrations on pages 46–48 are examples of molas made by young Cuna girls who are learning the craft. The girls' "practice" molas are not used for blouse panels but rather to satisfy the tourist trade.

The captions provide the Cuna name of the mola subject, when known, and its English equivalent. Also provided are the dimensions of the original molas from which the designs have been abstracted.

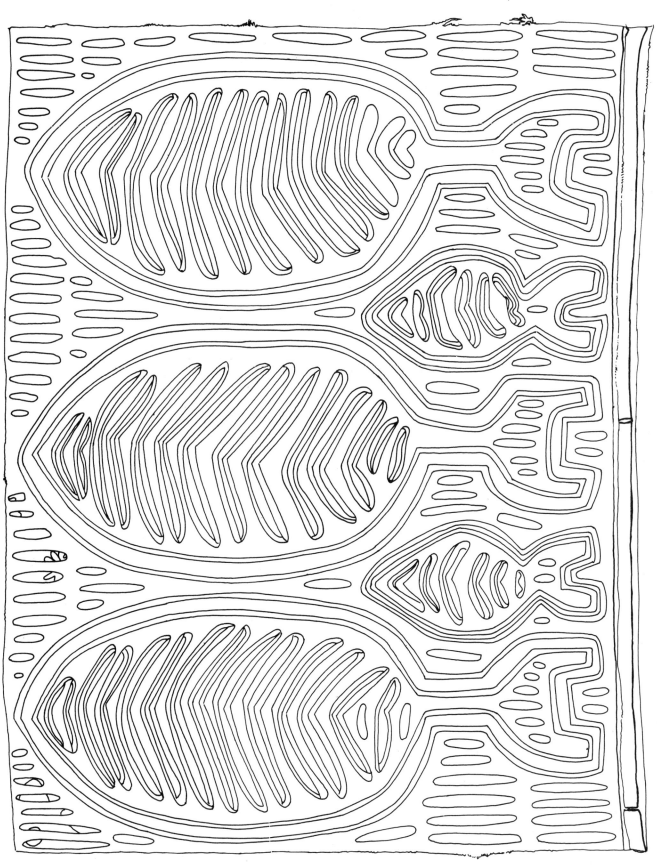

*Kami* (weaving paddle), 21″ × 17″.

*Nasis* (gourd rattle), 18¼" × 14¾".

Child's dress, 17½" × 16".

*Tibur* (calabash water scoop or cup), 18½″ × 15½″.

*Kurgin* (hat), 19″ × 14½″.

11

*Nacruz* (cruciform), 21″ × 17″. This design motif antedates the arrival of the Spaniards and the introduction of Christianity to the Americas.

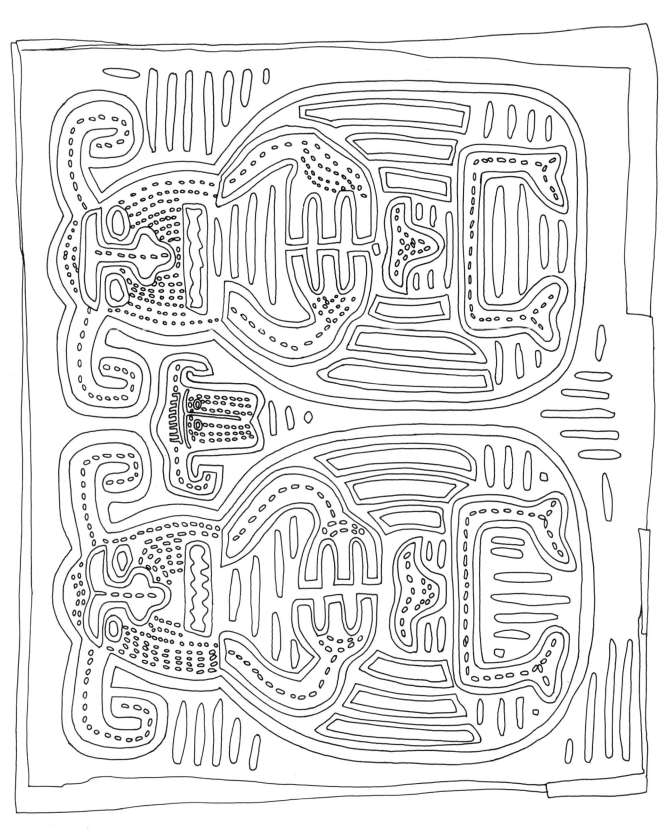

Ritual figures, 16″ × 13½″.

13

*Cristo rojo* (red Christ), 20″ × 15″.

*Waka nono* (stranger's head), 18¼″ × 14¾″.

*Uakala* (fish skeletons), 21″ × 15″.

*Sikwi* (birds), 14½" × 12½".

*Sug* (crab), *sikwi* (bird), and *karpa* (basket), 18½″ × 16¼″.

*Wekko* (bird pouncing on reptile), 19″ × 14½″.

19

*Sikwi* (bird) on back of an *achu* (dog). Corner objects, clockwise from upper left of illustration: *nali* (shark), an unknown object, a *sulu* (monkey), and a *sikwi* (bird). 18½" × 16".

Animal hunt, 18½″ × 15¾″.

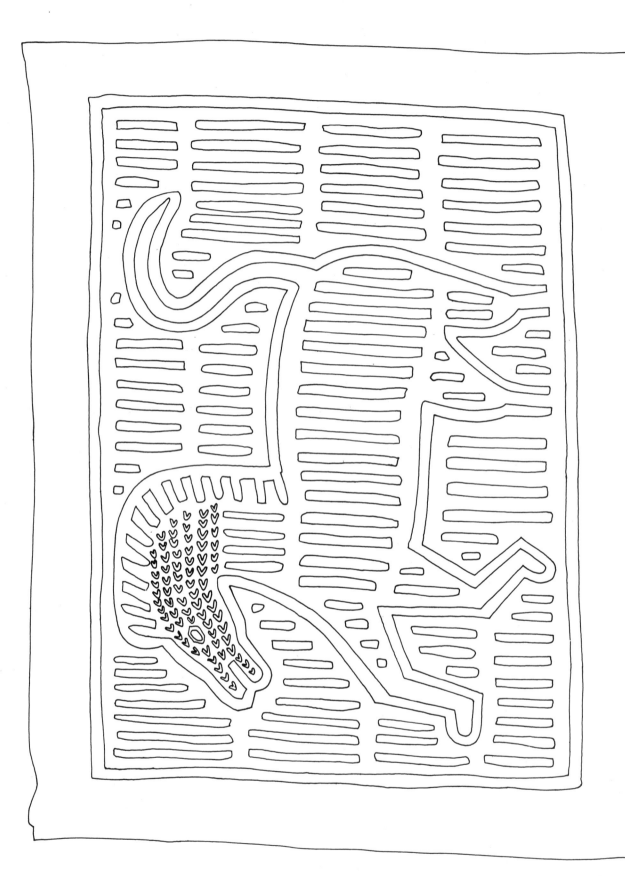

*Moli* (horse), 17¾" × 14".

*Sikwi* (bird) and *tuttu* (flower), 15" × 12¾".

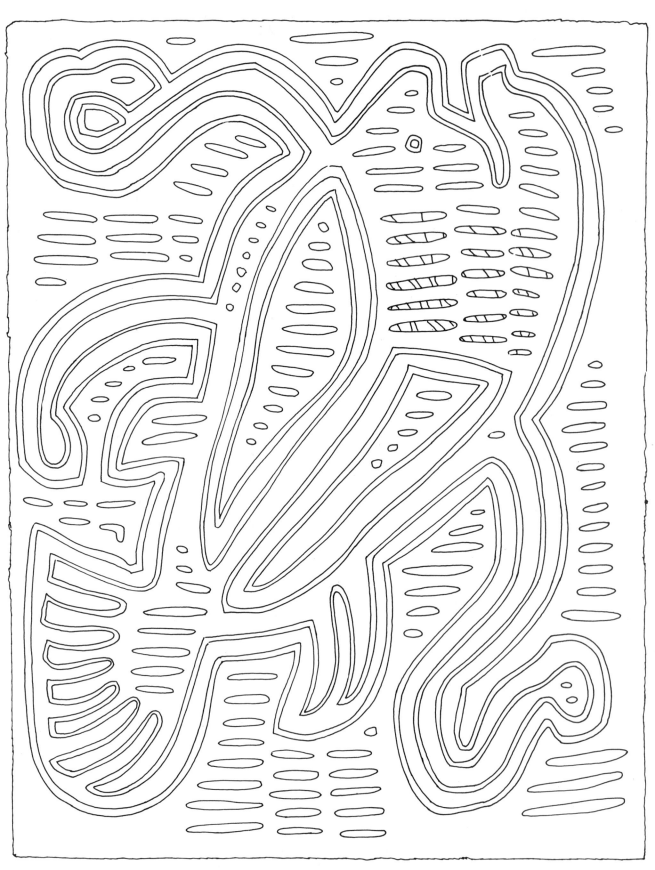

*Nitirbi* (devilfish), 17½" × 14".

*Misi* (cat), 20¼″ × 16″.

*Suchu* (butterfly), 18″ × 14″.

*Suchu* (butterfly), 20¼" × 18".

x

27

*Nitirbi* (devilfish), 16″ × 21¼″.

*Sikwi* (bird), 18″ × 16¼″.

*Sapi* (tree), 18" × 16".

*Tuttu* (flower form), 17¾" × 16".

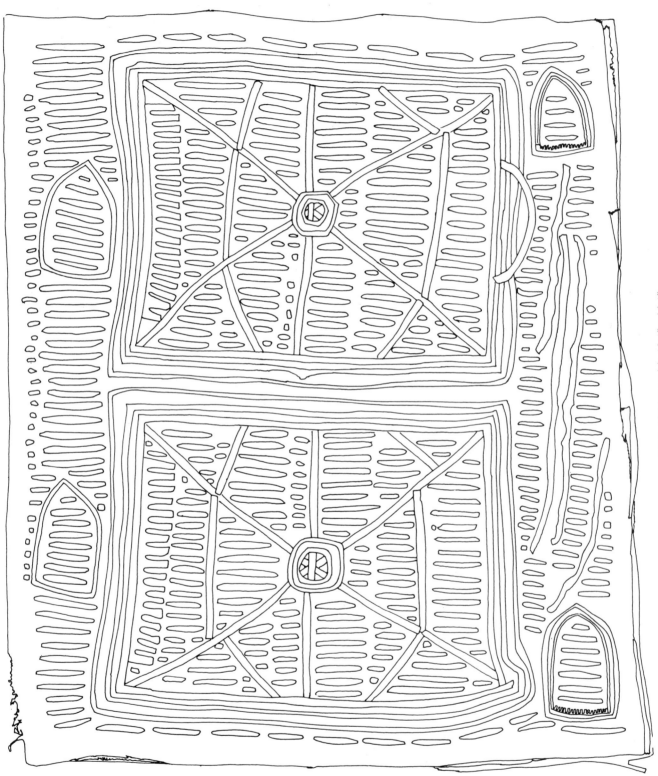

*Miria* (fishing weir), 19½″ × 14½″.

Double letter *M*, 17″ × 15¼″.

*Niskwa* (star), 19″ × 13¾″.

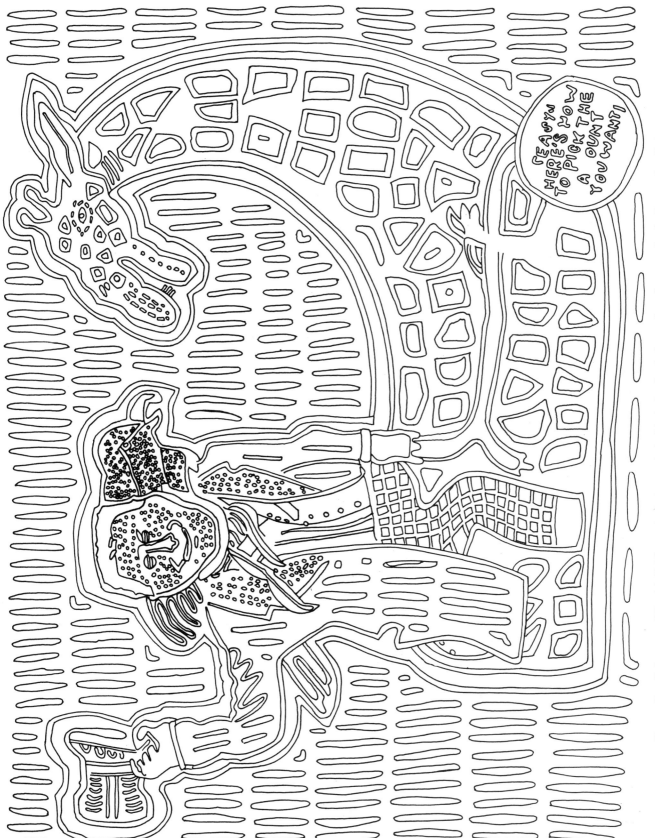

Doctor Doolittle game, 18″ × 14½″. The mola-maker copied this design freely from a box that contained a Doctor Doolittle game. The Doctor carries his parrot on his shoulder and rides a giraffe.

*Bander* (flag), 20″ × 15¾″.

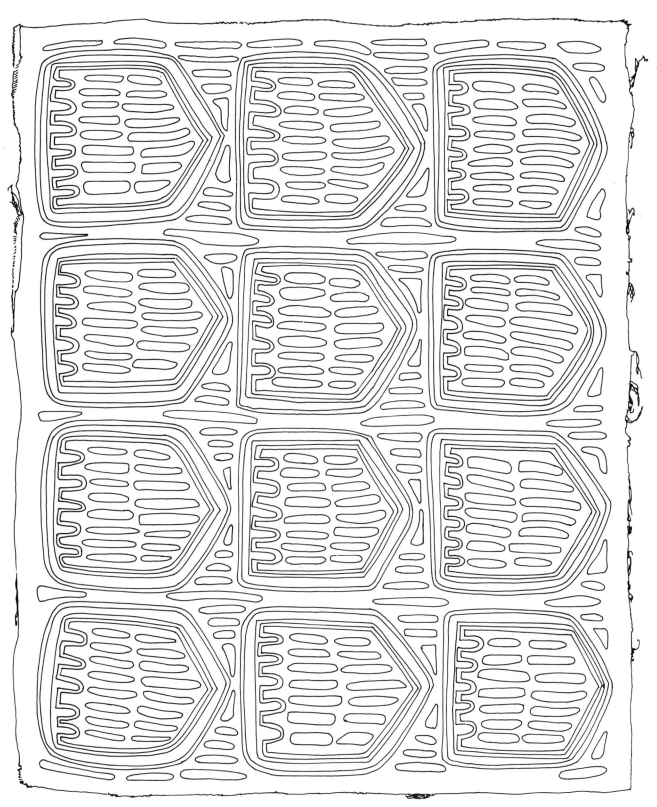

Shield pattern, 19½" × 16".

Maze design, 13" × 10".

Maze design, 13¾″ × 11½″.

Maze design, 13″ × 11½″.

Maze design, 16¾″ × 13½″.

Maze design, 13¾″ × 12½″.

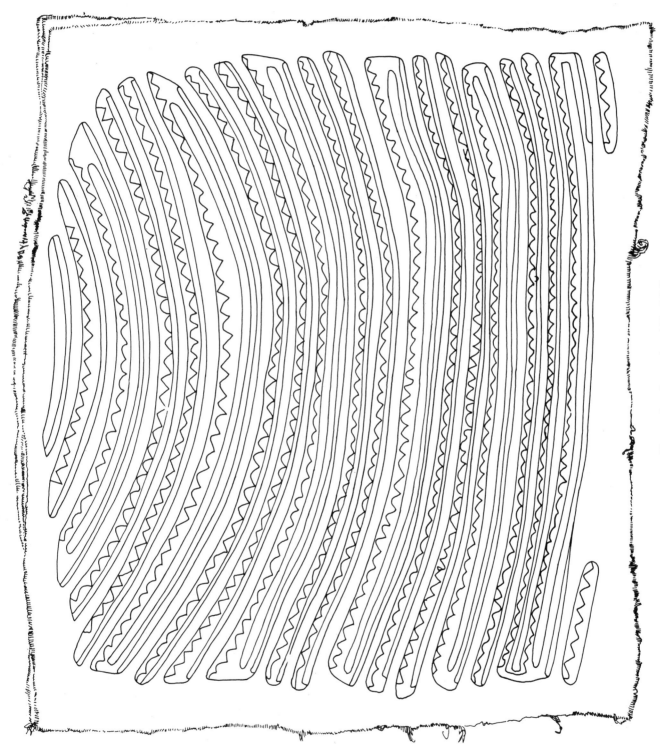

Decorative abstraction, 18″ × 15¾″.

Abstract form, 17" × 16".

Abstract form, 18" × 16½".

45

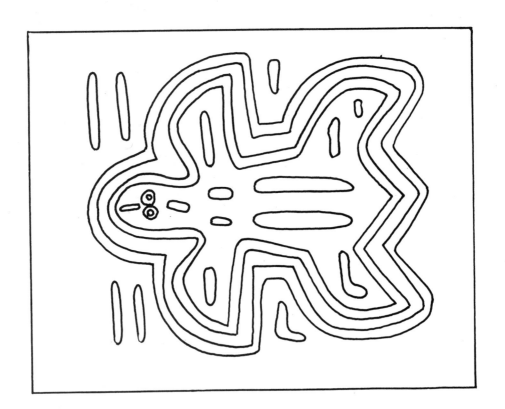

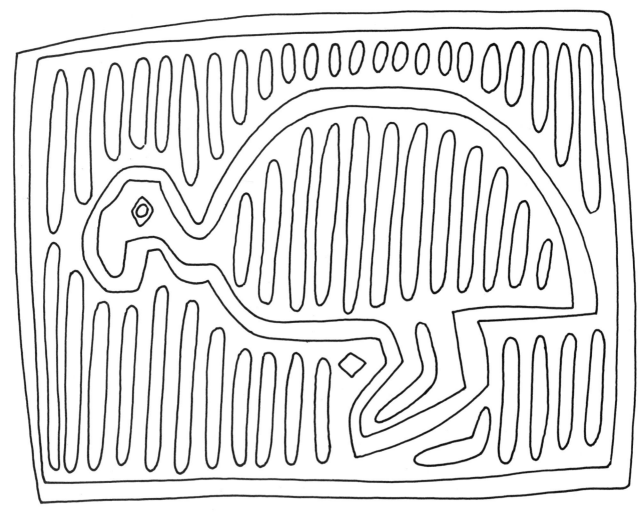

TOP: *Yauk* (baby sea turtle), 4⅝″ × 5⅝″.
BOTTOM: *Sikli* (turkey), 10″ × 8″.

TOP: *Kwili* (parrot), 6¾″ × 6″.
BOTTOM: *Kwile* (dancers), 9″ × 7½″

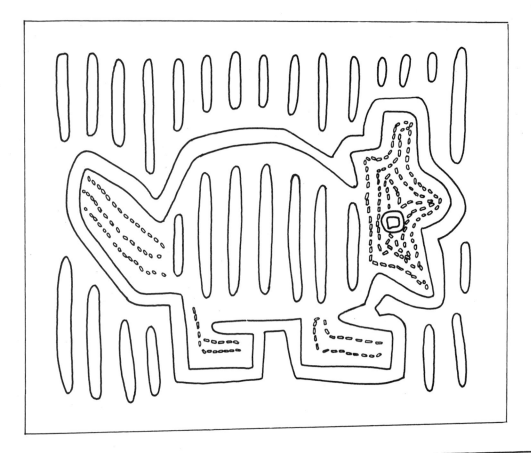

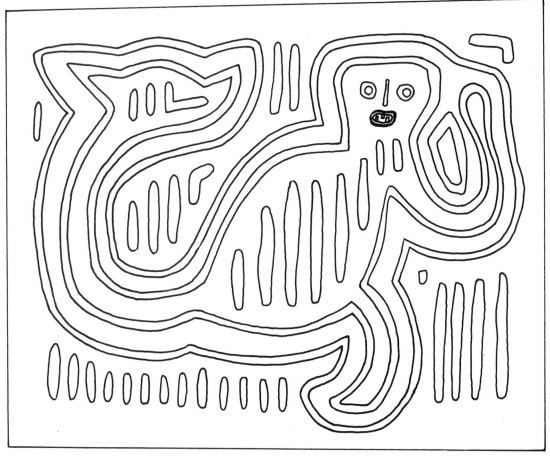

TOP: *Ukswini* (squirrel), 7¾" × 6¾".
BOTTOM: *Ansu* (mermaid), 9¼" × 7½".